REMEDY

LINDSEY GRAELER

authorHOUSE®

AuthorHouse™
1663 Liberty Drive
Bloomington, IN 47403
www.authorhouse.com
Phone: 833-262-8899

Published by AuthorHouse 02/08/2021

ISBN: 978-1-6655-1616-7 (sc)
ISBN: 978-1-6655-1615-0 (e)

Library of Congress Control Number: 2021902489

Print information available on the last page.

Any people depicted in stock imagery provided by Getty Images are models, and such images are being used for illustrative purposes only.
Certain stock imagery © Getty Images.

This book is printed on acid-free paper.

To the sludge in your gut and the fire in your ass.

To someone comfortable in their skin and someone who finds it a prison.

To someone who can't get out of bed and someone doing anything to avoid it.

To someone trusting the process and to someone thinking it's a narc.

To someone falling madly in love and someone who has no idea what that is.

To someone detached and to someone present.

To someone figuring it the fuck out and going through their trauma the best they can.

To anyone.

Let me
in world.

I am

your

OYSTER.

1

Someday

The peaches
are dead,
my silence
is louder.

The world is
round so I can
spin. flat, if
I'm in a hurry.

I lost you
because I've
never had anything

Two

No Outlet
I took one
look at that red
bush and had the
answers for the
day.

I put sex and
booze on a canvas.
Starving artist.
It sold for the
price of my soul.

I look in the
mirror and see
My Mom.
Three

Forrest Green

I built a tent
full of anger.

I forgot I
was camping.

When I tried
to go inside,
it broke.

I find this
tent useless.

I slept under
a tree.

four

I trace my beautiful
body in the shadows
and see no reason to
have it.

I ate something sweet
to feel sick.

I choose to lie in dirt
because I'm comfortable.

I'm the monster under
the bed, let me lie
and keep you fed.

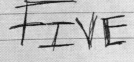

you

can

not

hurt

because you
are

hurting.

six

I write
to make
sense of
a world
that confused
me.

Probably not
for me
to understand.

SEVEN

I have never
felt like
I've had a
real home.

So I made
One in my
head.

eight

Femm bot

Lets drink pink
Wine and talk about
dicks.

Never wore eyeliner
by choice.

Our landlord said
I would be a dyke.
Not liking things
doesn't give you a
personality.

I want armpit hair
but I stink!

NINE

PAIN

I cry to the trees.

as if they've never
felt pain.

two deaths in two
years and my head is
throbbing.

I've _run_ myself dry,

I feel my flesh evaporate.

uncomfortable and motionless.

I'm trying to build a person
In my brain who
Can deal with this.

I miss my heart.

TEN

Funny Girl

You were not proud
of me.

I was a cute distraction
from yourself, I was willing
    to drain for that.

I felt like an accesory.

I am not a saint.
I am not easy.
I have wounds given and built.

I stand looking at a warm
empty hole trying to stay alive.

I will realize loss,
    but wake up and find my worth.

eleven

Alone

Everyday is different,

I went through my sock
drawer and it's like a
graveyard.

Sometimes I think about
how love heals and fucks
us up at the same time.

lets drink cheap beer
and talk about our feelings.

We take words, form them.

but in reality can we ever
really trust anything? That
big pink walnut is <u>also</u> my
enemy.

TWELVE

Garbage Voodoo

They hide it in
White smiles. Aesthetics
So you feel less vile.

Buy it for a
temporary fix.

Fuck it to feel.

The lack of love
is decaying my brain.

I put a fresh cream
elixir on to hide my
purple bags.

Beauty is nothing

Without Substance,

We all pay a price.

thirteen

Little Woman, who are you?

You don't know why life
is hard, me either.

You don't know why people
are dark, I do.

Even a black-eyed Susan
needs attention from the wild.

Every pretty girls a flower
          till she dies from no
water, sun, and a simple caress
of the petal, because admiring her
          was enough —
How do we get to a point
where beauty

and desire coincide

Without killing someone
barely alive?

Fourteen

You're a star ★

They call me the
fuck up,

The black sheep,

always two steps

backwards.

My hopes and dreams
are all they will
be.

I hope one day the
worms enjoy that I
never sold out.

15

Pleasant

My jaw is swollen
and I'm tired of
seeing kites.

Cheap fruit for my pie.

My smartest thought made
me dumb.

If I float by in my
silk robe would man
let me live another day?

Pink skulls,

plastic rose,

I'll hug this monster.

16

Cinnamon and Sugar

My feet off the
patio this Morning
but I wasn't that
scared.

I have this feeling
wrapped in pink bubbles.

I Keep my hips wide
so I don't waste space.

running in circles at
my favorite pace.

The moon is yellow and
I'm a howlin wolf.

17

Harder

I wouldn't look me
in the eyes anymore.

Do you think dust
  appears when
    you have nothing
    left?

  Giving up on trying
      so hard
      to end up with
      nothing.

  Use me.

  tear me open.

Suck me up through
a metal straw claiming
to change the world.

19

Onyx

Depression pudding.

I'm realizing the release,

the pressure is an imaginary
      balloon I've filled with bullshit.

I'm throwing up pink today.

That is how I express my feminine
      side.

Nothing is wrong, nothing is right.

Dance with me until it's dark.

20

I lost everything.

To realize it's not mine.

21

Two broken pieces

Should we blame the moon
for making the warmth we have
        a lovely seduction?

Damaged, tired, yet soulful eyes.

The softer the touch, the harder
        we fall.

One day the bombs go off in our

heads and we destroy that bliss.

Two broken pieces confused at
why they don't fit.
        Vacate.

    22   love the magician.

Time

A year,
Why does it hit harder?

an   hour,
We still have
time.

breath easier
Someday.

heal.

My heart lives in a swamp
listening to CCR.

23

Chuparosa

Brown eyed gypsy girl,
likes peanuts in her icecream.
You can't give her what she
needs.

She took a train to Texas,
Soon she'll be in Acapulco.

The bombs go off in her
brain and light up her toes.

She thinks about her
flaws and says

Damn I'm beautiful.

24

Charlie

Burgundy rivers.

The mole on
her left ear
makes me smile.

The wind is her friend.

I'm just an acquaintance.

that yellow dress.

Asking to borrow her

toothbrush makes
me whole.

25

Circles

I whimper softly into
my whole existence.

Craving something no
one can give me.

hang me out to dry
the air might know.

my feet are dirty,
good morning sunshine.

2/6

Calm down

I think if the wind
could speak to me it
call me a bastard.

The road feels less
rocky when you don't
give a shit!

The waters luke warm
and the sun is staring
at me.

I think about these
times, and feel like
this is what it means
to be alive.

27

September

Curtains are dropping.

My heart feels
like a balloon.

My mind is a fucking
Circus.

heavy.

28

HITCHHIKER

Queen of trash.
beatnik Cleopatra.

lighter in the dark.

Her life has no
purpose but her purpose
is life.

She thrives in disruption.

Stomach aches, slowly
this is her
normal.

What can you show her
that she hasn't
seen?

29

Expressions of Sympathy

All my life I have seen
Sadness in the prettiest
eyes.

I look at this body of water.
Sometimes I see silver.
Sometimes I see brown.

I have made choices out of
anger and fear because I'm
just a woman.

lonliness and ego,
the strongest drink.

I'm learning to forgive my
flesh.
Giving my heart and soul
freedom to find it's
home.   30

Exit

Cauldron brain.

I'm feeling a sense of
            security in my
       madness.

False prophet.

You have no power.

My jaw is wide and I
    could destroy you with

        a single hiss.

31

Funny Bone

Hearing my voice,
makes it feel
like Caramel.

I melt into my own
distractions.

The ice is thin for
my excitement.

Why did I waste my
time crying raindrops?

32

CANNARY YELLOW

This color makes me want to bathe in it.
Skip into the oblivious.
A tiny poet with tiny muscles.
I will eat the world, chew it up, spit it out, and make my peace.

33

Printed in the United States
By Bookmasters